50 Premium Breakfast French Dishes

By: Kelly Johnson

Table of Contents

- Croissant aux Amandes (Almond Croissant)
- Pain Perdu (French Toast)
- Quiche Lorraine
- Oeufs Bénédicte (Eggs Benedict)
- Croque-Madame
- Brioche à Tête
- Tarte Tatin aux Pommes (Apple Tarte Tatin)
- Crêpes Suzette
- Omelette aux Fines Herbes
- Chaussons aux Pommes (Apple Turnovers)
- Baguette avec Beurre et Confiture
- Clafoutis aux Cerises (Cherry Clafoutis)
- Kouign-Amann
- Gaufres à la Vanille (Vanilla Waffles)
- Madeleine au Citron (Lemon Madeleines)
- Galette des Rois
- Soufflé au Fromage (Cheese Soufflé)
- Pains aux Raisins
- Chocolatine (Pain au Chocolat)
- Tartine Beurrée avec Miel
- Crêpes au Chocolat et Noisettes
- Gâteau de Riz à la Vanille
- Flan Parisien
- Roulé à la Cannelle (French Cinnamon Roll)
- Financier aux Amandes
- Beignets de Carnaval
- Muffins à la Framboise et au Chocolat Blanc
- Tarte aux Myrtilles (Blueberry Tart)
- Sablés Bretons (French Butter Cookies)
- Pain de Mie Maison
- Pommes de Terre Rissolées (French-Style Hash Browns)
- Pithiviers à la Crème d'Amande
- Mousse au Chocolat Matinale
- Navettes Provençales (Orange Blossom Cookies)
- Bostock (Brioche with Almond Cream)

- Gâteau Basque à la Crème
- Croissant Jambon-Fromage (Ham and Cheese Croissant)
- Pancakes à la Vanille et au Beurre Salé
- Riz au Lait avec Caramel Beurre Salé
- Fougasse aux Olives et Romarin
- Pain aux Noix et Figues
- Chouquettes au Sucre
- Tarte Tropézienne
- Viennoiseries Mixtes (Assorted Pastries)
- Tarte aux Abricots et Amandes
- Petits Pains au Lait
- Gâteau au Yaourt et Citron
- Porridge au Lait d'Amande et Miel
- Far Breton aux Pruneaux
- Salade de Fruits Frais avec Lavande

Croissant aux Amandes (Almond Croissant)

Ingredients:

- 4 day-old croissants
- 1/2 cup almond flour
- 1/4 cup sugar
- 2 tbsp butter, softened
- 1 egg
- 1/2 tsp vanilla extract
- 1/4 cup sliced almonds
- Powdered sugar for dusting

Instructions:

1. Preheat oven to 350°F (175°C).
2. Mix almond flour, sugar, butter, egg, and vanilla until smooth.
3. Slice croissants in half and spread almond filling inside and on top.
4. Sprinkle with sliced almonds and bake for 10-12 minutes.
5. Dust with powdered sugar before serving.

Pain Perdu (French Toast)

Ingredients:

- 4 thick slices of brioche or French bread
- 2 eggs
- 1/2 cup milk
- 1 tbsp sugar
- 1/2 tsp vanilla extract
- 1/2 tsp cinnamon
- Butter for frying

Instructions:

1. Whisk eggs, milk, sugar, vanilla, and cinnamon.
2. Dip bread slices in the mixture until soaked.
3. Heat butter in a pan and cook each slice for 2-3 minutes per side.
4. Serve with powdered sugar, syrup, or fresh fruit.

Quiche Lorraine

Ingredients:

- 1 pre-made pie crust
- 4 eggs
- 1 cup heavy cream
- 1/2 cup cooked bacon, chopped
- 1/2 cup grated Gruyère cheese
- 1/2 tsp salt
- 1/4 tsp black pepper

Instructions:

1. Preheat oven to 375°F (190°C).
2. Whisk eggs, cream, salt, and pepper.
3. Sprinkle bacon and cheese into the pie crust, then pour egg mixture over.
4. Bake for 35-40 minutes until set.

Oeufs Bénédicte (Eggs Benedict)

Ingredients:

Hollandaise Sauce:

- 2 egg yolks
- 1/2 cup butter, melted
- 1 tbsp lemon juice

Eggs Benedict:

- 2 English muffins, halved and toasted
- 4 poached eggs
- 4 slices ham

Instructions:

1. Blend egg yolks and lemon juice, then slowly drizzle in melted butter while blending until thickened.
2. Poach eggs in simmering water for 3-4 minutes.
3. Assemble with ham on muffins, top with eggs, and drizzle with hollandaise sauce.

Croque-Madame

Ingredients:

- 4 slices of brioche or white bread
- 2 tbsp butter
- 2 tbsp flour
- 1 cup milk
- 1/2 cup grated Gruyère cheese
- 4 slices ham
- 2 fried eggs

Instructions:

1. Melt butter in a pan, add flour, and whisk for 1 minute. Gradually add milk, stirring until thick.
2. Spread béchamel sauce on bread slices, top with ham and cheese, then grill in a pan until golden brown.
3. Serve with a fried egg on top.

Brioche à Tête

Ingredients:

- 3 cups flour
- 2 tbsp sugar
- 1/2 tsp salt
- 1 packet dry yeast
- 1/2 cup warm milk
- 3 eggs
- 1/2 cup butter, softened

Instructions:

1. Mix yeast with warm milk and let sit for 5 minutes.
2. Combine flour, sugar, salt, eggs, and yeast mixture. Knead until smooth.
3. Add butter and knead until elastic. Let rise for 2 hours.
4. Shape dough into small rounds, place in muffin tins, and let rise for another hour.
5. Bake at 375°F (190°C) for 15 minutes.

Tarte Tatin aux Pommes (Apple Tarte Tatin)

Ingredients:

- 4 apples, peeled and sliced
- 1/2 cup sugar
- 4 tbsp butter
- 1 sheet puff pastry

Instructions:

1. Preheat oven to 375°F (190°C).
2. Melt sugar and butter in a pan until caramelized, then add apples. Cook for 5 minutes.
3. Place puff pastry over the apples and tuck edges in.
4. Bake for 25 minutes. Invert onto a plate before serving.

Crêpes Suzette

Ingredients:

Crêpes:

- 1 cup flour
- 2 eggs
- 1 cup milk
- 1 tbsp sugar

Orange Sauce:

- 1/4 cup butter
- 1/4 cup sugar
- 1/2 cup orange juice
- 2 tbsp Grand Marnier

Instructions:

1. Whisk crêpe ingredients and let rest for 30 minutes.
2. Cook thin crêpes in a buttered pan.
3. For sauce, melt butter and sugar, then add orange juice and Grand Marnier. Simmer for 2 minutes.
4. Dip crêpes in sauce and fold before serving.

Omelette aux Fines Herbes

Ingredients:

- 3 eggs
- 1 tbsp milk
- 1 tbsp fresh herbs (chives, parsley, tarragon)
- Salt and black pepper to taste
- 1 tbsp butter

Instructions:

1. Whisk eggs, milk, herbs, salt, and pepper.
2. Melt butter in a pan, pour in eggs, and cook over low heat until set.
3. Fold and serve warm.

Chaussons aux Pommes (Apple Turnovers)

Ingredients:

- 1 sheet puff pastry
- 2 apples, peeled and diced
- 2 tbsp sugar
- 1/2 tsp cinnamon
- 1 tbsp butter

Instructions:

1. Sauté apples, sugar, cinnamon, and butter until soft.
2. Cut puff pastry into squares, add apple filling, and fold into triangles.
3. Bake at 375°F (190°C) for 20 minutes.

Baguette avec Beurre et Confiture

Ingredients:

- 1 fresh baguette
- 4 tbsp butter
- 1/4 cup jam (strawberry, raspberry, or apricot)

Instructions:

1. Slice baguette and spread with butter and jam.
2. Serve as a simple yet classic French breakfast or snack.

Clafoutis aux Cerises (Cherry Clafoutis)

Ingredients:

- 2 cups fresh cherries, pitted
- 3 eggs
- 1/2 cup sugar
- 1/2 cup flour
- 1 cup whole milk
- 1/2 cup heavy cream
- 1 tsp vanilla extract
- 1/4 tsp salt
- Powdered sugar for dusting

Instructions:

1. Preheat oven to 375°F (190°C). Butter a baking dish and spread cherries in the bottom.
2. Whisk eggs and sugar until light, then add flour, milk, cream, vanilla, and salt.
3. Pour batter over cherries and bake for 35-40 minutes until set.
4. Dust with powdered sugar before serving.

Kouign-Amann

Ingredients:

- 2 1/4 cups flour
- 1 tsp salt
- 2 1/4 tsp active dry yeast
- 3/4 cup warm water
- 1 cup butter, cold and diced
- 3/4 cup sugar

Instructions:

1. Mix flour, salt, yeast, and warm water into a dough. Let rise for 1 hour.
2. Roll out dough into a rectangle, place butter in the center, and fold into thirds.
3. Chill for 30 minutes, then roll out again, fold, and repeat 3 times.
4. Sprinkle with sugar, fold, and roll again.
5. Cut into squares, place in muffin tins, and bake at 375°F (190°C) for 30 minutes.

Gaufres à la Vanille (Vanilla Waffles)

Ingredients:

- 2 cups flour
- 2 tbsp sugar
- 1 tsp baking powder
- 1/2 tsp salt
- 2 eggs
- 1 3/4 cups milk
- 1/2 cup butter, melted
- 1 tsp vanilla extract

Instructions:

1. Preheat waffle iron.
2. Mix dry ingredients in one bowl. Whisk eggs, milk, butter, and vanilla in another.
3. Combine wet and dry ingredients and mix until smooth.
4. Pour batter into waffle iron and cook until golden brown.

Madeleine au Citron (Lemon Madeleines)

Ingredients:

- 2 eggs
- 1/2 cup sugar
- 1/2 cup flour
- 1/4 cup butter, melted
- 1 tsp lemon zest
- 1/2 tsp vanilla extract
- 1/2 tsp baking powder

Instructions:

1. Preheat oven to 375°F (190°C). Grease madeleine molds.
2. Whisk eggs and sugar until fluffy. Fold in flour, baking powder, lemon zest, and vanilla.
3. Add melted butter and mix gently.
4. Spoon batter into molds and bake for 10-12 minutes.

Galette des Rois

Ingredients:

- 2 sheets puff pastry
- 1/2 cup almond flour
- 1/4 cup sugar
- 2 tbsp butter, softened
- 1 egg
- 1/2 tsp vanilla extract
- 1 egg yolk (for glazing)

Instructions:

1. Preheat oven to 375°F (190°C).
2. Mix almond flour, sugar, butter, egg, and vanilla to make the filling.
3. Place one puff pastry sheet on a baking sheet, spread filling in the center, and cover with the second sheet.
4. Seal edges, brush with egg yolk, and bake for 25-30 minutes.

Soufflé au Fromage (Cheese Soufflé)

Ingredients:

- 2 tbsp butter
- 2 tbsp flour
- 1 cup milk
- 1/2 tsp salt
- 1/4 tsp black pepper
- 3 eggs, separated
- 1 cup grated Gruyère cheese

Instructions:

1. Preheat oven to 375°F (190°C). Grease a soufflé dish.
2. Melt butter, stir in flour, and cook for 1 minute. Slowly whisk in milk, salt, and pepper.
3. Remove from heat, mix in egg yolks and cheese.
4. Beat egg whites until stiff and fold into mixture.
5. Pour into dish and bake for 25-30 minutes until puffed and golden.

Pains aux Raisins

Ingredients:

- 1 sheet puff pastry
- 1/2 cup pastry cream
- 1/2 cup raisins
- 1 tbsp sugar
- 1 egg yolk

Instructions:

1. Preheat oven to 375°F (190°C). Roll out puff pastry into a rectangle.
2. Spread pastry cream over dough and sprinkle with raisins.
3. Roll up tightly and slice into rounds.
4. Place on a baking sheet, brush with egg yolk, and bake for 20 minutes.

Chocolatine (Pain au Chocolat)

Ingredients:

- 1 sheet puff pastry
- 2 chocolate bars
- 1 egg yolk

Instructions:

1. Cut puff pastry into rectangles.
2. Place a chocolate bar on each and roll up tightly.
3. Place seam-side down on a baking sheet, brush with egg yolk, and bake at 375°F (190°C) for 15 minutes.

Tartine Beurrée avec Miel

Ingredients:

- 1 fresh baguette
- 2 tbsp butter
- 2 tbsp honey

Instructions:

1. Slice baguette and spread with butter.
2. Drizzle with honey and serve.

Crêpes au Chocolat et Noisettes (Chocolate and Hazelnut Crêpes)

Ingredients:

- 1 cup flour
- 2 tbsp cocoa powder
- 2 tbsp sugar
- 1 1/4 cups milk
- 2 eggs
- 2 tbsp melted butter
- 1/2 tsp vanilla extract
- 1/2 cup hazelnut spread
- 1/4 cup chopped toasted hazelnuts

Instructions:

1. Whisk flour, cocoa powder, sugar, milk, eggs, butter, and vanilla until smooth. Let rest for 30 minutes.
2. Heat a non-stick pan over medium heat and cook thin crêpes for 1-2 minutes per side.
3. Spread hazelnut spread over each crêpe, sprinkle with hazelnuts, and fold or roll before serving.

Gâteau de Riz à la Vanille (Vanilla Rice Pudding Cake)

Ingredients:

- 1/2 cup Arborio rice
- 2 cups milk
- 1/4 cup sugar
- 1 tsp vanilla extract
- 2 eggs
- 1/4 cup raisins (optional)
- Butter for greasing

Instructions:

1. Preheat oven to 350°F (175°C).
2. Cook rice in milk over low heat until creamy (about 20 minutes).
3. Stir in sugar and vanilla. Let cool slightly, then mix in beaten eggs and raisins.
4. Pour into a greased baking dish and bake for 30 minutes.

Flan Parisien (Parisian Custard Tart)

Ingredients:

- 2 cups whole milk
- 1/2 cup heavy cream
- 1/2 cup sugar
- 3 tbsp cornstarch
- 3 egg yolks
- 1 tsp vanilla extract
- 1 sheet puff pastry

Instructions:

1. Preheat oven to 375°F (190°C).
2. Heat milk and cream in a saucepan. Whisk egg yolks, sugar, and cornstarch separately.
3. Slowly pour hot milk into the egg mixture, whisking constantly. Return to heat and stir until thickened.
4. Line a tart pan with puff pastry and pour in custard.
5. Bake for 35-40 minutes until set and golden brown.

Roulé à la Cannelle (French Cinnamon Roll)

Ingredients:

Dough:

- 2 1/2 cups flour
- 1/4 cup sugar
- 1 tsp salt
- 2 1/4 tsp dry yeast
- 3/4 cup warm milk
- 1 egg
- 1/4 cup butter, melted

Filling:

- 1/2 cup brown sugar
- 2 tbsp cinnamon
- 2 tbsp butter, melted

Instructions:

1. Mix yeast with warm milk and let sit for 5 minutes. Add flour, sugar, salt, egg, and butter. Knead into dough and let rise for 1 hour.
2. Roll out dough into a rectangle, brush with melted butter, and sprinkle with cinnamon sugar.
3. Roll up tightly and slice into rolls. Place in a baking dish and let rise for another 30 minutes.
4. Bake at 375°F (190°C) for 20 minutes.

Financier aux Amandes (Almond Financiers)

Ingredients:

- 1/2 cup almond flour
- 1/2 cup powdered sugar
- 1/4 cup flour
- 1/4 tsp salt
- 3 egg whites
- 1/4 cup melted butter
- 1/2 tsp vanilla extract

Instructions:

1. Preheat oven to 375°F (190°C).
2. Mix almond flour, powdered sugar, flour, and salt. Stir in egg whites, butter, and vanilla.
3. Pour batter into small molds and bake for 12-15 minutes.

Beignets de Carnaval (French Carnival Doughnuts)

Ingredients:

- 2 cups flour
- 1/4 cup sugar
- 1/2 tsp salt
- 2 eggs
- 1/2 cup milk
- 2 tbsp butter, melted
- 1 tsp vanilla extract
- Oil for frying
- Powdered sugar for dusting

Instructions:

1. Mix flour, sugar, and salt. Stir in eggs, milk, butter, and vanilla. Knead into a soft dough and let rest for 30 minutes.
2. Roll out dough and cut into small rectangles.
3. Fry in hot oil at 350°F (175°C) until golden brown. Drain and dust with powdered sugar.

Muffins à la Framboise et au Chocolat Blanc (Raspberry and White Chocolate Muffins)

Ingredients:

- 1 1/2 cups flour
- 1/2 cup sugar
- 1/2 tsp baking powder
- 1/4 tsp salt
- 1/2 cup milk
- 1/4 cup butter, melted
- 1 egg
- 1/2 cup raspberries
- 1/4 cup white chocolate chips

Instructions:

1. Preheat oven to 375°F (190°C).
2. Mix flour, sugar, baking powder, and salt. Stir in milk, butter, and egg.
3. Gently fold in raspberries and white chocolate chips.
4. Spoon into muffin tins and bake for 18-20 minutes.

Tarte aux Myrtilles (Blueberry Tart)

Ingredients:

Crust:

- 1 1/4 cups flour
- 1/2 cup butter, cubed
- 1/4 cup sugar
- 1 egg yolk

Filling:

- 2 cups fresh blueberries
- 1/4 cup sugar
- 1 tbsp cornstarch
- 1/2 tsp lemon zest

Instructions:

1. Preheat oven to 375°F (190°C). Mix crust ingredients and press into a tart pan. Bake for 10 minutes.
2. Mix blueberries, sugar, cornstarch, and lemon zest. Pour into crust.
3. Bake for 20-25 minutes.

Sablés Bretons (French Butter Cookies)

Ingredients:

- 1 cup flour
- 1/2 cup butter, softened
- 1/4 cup sugar
- 1 egg yolk
- 1/2 tsp vanilla extract
- 1/4 tsp salt

Instructions:

1. Preheat oven to 350°F (175°C).
2. Mix flour, butter, sugar, egg yolk, vanilla, and salt into a dough.
3. Roll out and cut into circles. Place on a baking sheet and bake for 12-15 minutes.

Pain de Mie Maison (French Sandwich Bread)

Ingredients:

- 3 cups flour
- 1 tbsp sugar
- 1 1/2 tsp salt
- 2 1/4 tsp dry yeast
- 3/4 cup warm milk
- 1/4 cup butter, melted
- 1 egg

Instructions:

1. Mix yeast with warm milk and sugar. Let sit for 5 minutes.
2. Stir in flour, salt, butter, and egg. Knead until smooth. Let rise for 1 hour.
3. Shape into a loaf and place in a greased bread pan. Let rise for another 30 minutes.
4. Bake at 375°F (190°C) for 25-30 minutes.

Pommes de Terre Rissolées (French-Style Hash Browns)

Ingredients:

- 4 medium potatoes, peeled and diced
- 2 tbsp butter
- 1 tbsp olive oil
- 1 clove garlic, minced
- 1/2 tsp salt
- 1/4 tsp black pepper
- 1 tbsp chopped parsley

Instructions:

1. Parboil diced potatoes in salted water for 5 minutes, then drain and pat dry.
2. Heat butter and olive oil in a pan over medium heat.
3. Add potatoes and cook for 10-15 minutes, stirring occasionally, until golden brown.
4. Stir in garlic, salt, and pepper. Cook for 2 more minutes.
5. Sprinkle with parsley before serving.

Pithiviers à la Crème d'Amande (Almond Cream Pithiviers)

Ingredients:

- 2 sheets puff pastry
- 1/2 cup almond flour
- 1/4 cup sugar
- 2 tbsp butter, softened
- 1 egg
- 1/2 tsp vanilla extract
- 1 egg yolk (for glazing)

Instructions:

1. Preheat oven to 375°F (190°C).
2. Mix almond flour, sugar, butter, egg, and vanilla to make the almond cream.
3. Cut puff pastry into two circles. Spread almond cream on one, leaving a border.
4. Cover with the second pastry circle and press edges to seal.
5. Brush with egg yolk and bake for 25-30 minutes.

Mousse au Chocolat Matinale

Ingredients:

- 4 oz dark chocolate
- 2 eggs, separated
- 2 tbsp sugar
- 1/2 cup heavy cream
- 1/2 tsp vanilla extract

Instructions:

1. Melt chocolate and let cool slightly.
2. Whisk egg yolks and sugar until pale, then stir into chocolate.
3. Beat egg whites until stiff, and separately whip cream until thick.
4. Fold egg whites and whipped cream into the chocolate mixture.
5. Chill for 2 hours before serving.

Navettes Provençales (Orange Blossom Cookies)

Ingredients:

- 2 cups flour
- 1/2 cup sugar
- 1/4 cup olive oil
- 1/4 cup milk
- 1 tbsp orange blossom water
- 1/2 tsp baking powder
- 1 egg

Instructions:

1. Preheat oven to 350°F (175°C).
2. Mix flour, sugar, and baking powder. Stir in olive oil, milk, orange blossom water, and egg.
3. Knead into a dough, then shape into small boats.
4. Bake for 15-18 minutes.

Bostock (Brioche with Almond Cream)

Ingredients:

- 4 slices of brioche
- 1/2 cup almond flour
- 1/4 cup sugar
- 2 tbsp butter, softened
- 1 egg
- 1/2 tsp vanilla extract
- 1/4 cup sliced almonds
- Powdered sugar for dusting

Instructions:

1. Preheat oven to 375°F (190°C).
2. Mix almond flour, sugar, butter, egg, and vanilla.
3. Spread almond cream on brioche slices and top with sliced almonds.
4. Bake for 12-15 minutes. Dust with powdered sugar before serving.

Gâteau Basque à la Crème

Ingredients:

Pastry:

- 2 cups flour
- 1/2 cup sugar
- 1/2 cup butter, softened
- 1 egg
- 1/2 tsp baking powder
- 1/2 tsp vanilla extract

Filling:

- 1 cup milk
- 2 egg yolks
- 1/4 cup sugar
- 2 tbsp cornstarch
- 1/2 tsp vanilla extract

Instructions:

1. Preheat oven to 375°F (190°C).
2. Mix pastry ingredients into a dough and refrigerate for 30 minutes.
3. Heat milk, then whisk yolks, sugar, cornstarch, and vanilla separately. Gradually mix with milk and cook until thick.
4. Roll out half the dough in a tart pan, pour in custard, then cover with remaining dough.
5. Bake for 30 minutes.

Croissant Jambon-Fromage (Ham and Cheese Croissant)

Ingredients:

- 4 croissants
- 4 slices ham
- 4 slices Gruyère cheese
- 2 tbsp Dijon mustard

Instructions:

1. Preheat oven to 350°F (175°C).
2. Slice croissants open and spread Dijon mustard inside.
3. Add ham and cheese, then bake for 5-7 minutes until cheese melts.

Pancakes à la Vanille et au Beurre Salé

Ingredients:

- 1 1/2 cups flour
- 1 tbsp sugar
- 1 tsp baking powder
- 1/2 tsp salt
- 1 1/4 cups milk
- 1 egg
- 1 tbsp melted butter
- 1 tsp vanilla extract
- 2 tbsp salted butter, for serving

Instructions:

1. Mix flour, sugar, baking powder, and salt.
2. In another bowl, whisk milk, egg, melted butter, and vanilla.
3. Stir wet ingredients into dry ingredients.
4. Cook pancakes in a buttered pan for 2 minutes per side.
5. Serve with salted butter and syrup.

Riz au Lait avec Caramel Beurre Salé

Ingredients:

Rice Pudding:

- 1/2 cup Arborio rice
- 2 cups milk
- 1/4 cup sugar
- 1/2 tsp vanilla extract

Salted Caramel:

- 1/2 cup sugar
- 2 tbsp butter
- 1/4 cup heavy cream
- 1/4 tsp sea salt

Instructions:

1. Simmer rice, milk, sugar, and vanilla until creamy (about 20 minutes).
2. For caramel, melt sugar in a saucepan, add butter, then stir in cream and salt.

3. Serve rice pudding with a drizzle of salted caramel.

Fougasse aux Olives et Romarin

Ingredients:

- 3 cups flour
- 1 tsp salt
- 1 packet dry yeast
- 3/4 cup warm water
- 2 tbsp olive oil
- 1/2 cup black olives, sliced
- 1 tbsp fresh rosemary

Instructions:

1. Mix yeast with warm water and let sit for 5 minutes.
2. Stir in flour, salt, olive oil, olives, and rosemary. Knead until smooth.
3. Let dough rise for 1 hour, then shape into a leaf with slits.
4. Bake at 400°F (200°C) for 20-25 minutes.

Pain aux Noix et Figues (Walnut and Fig Bread)

Ingredients:

- 3 cups flour
- 1 packet dry yeast
- 1 cup warm water
- 1 tsp salt
- 1 tbsp honey
- 1/2 cup dried figs, chopped
- 1/2 cup walnuts, chopped

Instructions:

1. Dissolve yeast in warm water with honey and let sit for 5 minutes.
2. Mix flour and salt, then add yeast mixture, kneading until smooth.
3. Fold in figs and walnuts. Let rise for 1 hour.
4. Shape into a loaf, let rise for another 30 minutes, then bake at 375°F (190°C) for 25-30 minutes.

Chouquettes au Sucre (French Sugar Puffs)

Ingredients:

- 1/2 cup water
- 1/2 cup milk
- 1/4 cup butter
- 1 tbsp sugar
- 1/2 tsp salt
- 1 cup flour
- 4 eggs
- 1/4 cup pearl sugar

Instructions:

1. Preheat oven to 375°F (190°C).
2. Heat water, milk, butter, sugar, and salt until melted. Stir in flour and cook for 1 minute.
3. Remove from heat and beat in eggs one at a time.

4. Pipe small rounds onto a baking sheet, sprinkle with pearl sugar, and bake for 20-25 minutes.

Tarte Tropézienne (Brioche Cream Tart)

Ingredients:

Brioche:

- 2 cups flour
- 1/4 cup sugar
- 1/2 tsp salt
- 1 packet dry yeast
- 1/2 cup warm milk
- 2 eggs
- 1/4 cup butter, softened

Filling:

- 1 cup heavy cream
- 1/2 cup pastry cream
- 1 tbsp sugar
- 1/2 tsp vanilla extract

Instructions:

1. Mix yeast with warm milk and let sit. Combine flour, sugar, salt, eggs, and yeast mixture. Knead in butter. Let rise for 1 hour.
2. Shape into a round and bake at 350°F (175°C) for 20 minutes.
3. Whip cream with pastry cream, sugar, and vanilla. Slice brioche in half and fill with cream.

Viennoiseries Mixtes (Assorted Pastries)

Ingredients:

- 1 sheet puff pastry
- 1/2 cup pastry cream
- 1/4 cup chocolate chips
- 1/4 cup sliced almonds
- 1 tbsp sugar

Instructions:

1. Cut puff pastry into small rectangles.
2. Fill some with pastry cream, others with chocolate chips, and sprinkle some with almonds.
3. Fold or roll, place on a baking sheet, and bake at 375°F (190°C) for 15-20 minutes.

Tarte aux Abricots et Amandes (Apricot and Almond Tart)

Ingredients:

Crust:

- 1 1/4 cups flour
- 1/2 cup butter
- 1/4 cup sugar
- 1 egg yolk

Filling:

- 1/2 cup almond flour
- 1/4 cup sugar
- 2 tbsp butter, softened
- 1 egg
- 6 apricots, halved

Instructions:

1. Preheat oven to 375°F (190°C). Mix crust ingredients and press into a tart pan. Bake for 10 minutes.
2. Mix almond flour, sugar, butter, and egg. Spread over crust.
3. Arrange apricots on top and bake for 25 minutes.

Petits Pains au Lait (Soft Milk Rolls)

Ingredients:

- 3 cups flour
- 1 packet dry yeast
- 1/2 cup warm milk
- 1/4 cup sugar
- 1/4 cup butter, melted
- 1 egg
- 1/2 tsp salt

Instructions:

1. Mix yeast with warm milk and sugar. Let sit for 5 minutes.
2. Stir in flour, salt, butter, and egg. Knead into dough and let rise for 1 hour.
3. Shape into small rolls, let rise again, then bake at 375°F (190°C) for 15 minutes.

Gâteau au Yaourt et Citron (Lemon Yogurt Cake)

Ingredients:

- 1 cup plain yogurt
- 1 cup sugar
- 1/2 cup vegetable oil
- 2 eggs
- 1 1/2 cups flour
- 1 tsp baking powder
- Zest of 1 lemon

Instructions:

1. Preheat oven to 350°F (175°C).
2. Whisk yogurt, sugar, oil, and eggs. Stir in flour, baking powder, and lemon zest.
3. Pour into a greased loaf pan and bake for 30-35 minutes.

Porridge au Lait d'Amande et Miel (Almond Milk and Honey Porridge)

Ingredients:

- 1/2 cup rolled oats
- 1 cup almond milk
- 1 tbsp honey
- 1/4 tsp cinnamon

Instructions:

1. Simmer oats in almond milk for 5 minutes.
2. Stir in honey and cinnamon before serving.

Far Breton aux Pruneaux (Brittany Prune Flan)

Ingredients:

- 1/2 cup prunes
- 1 cup flour
- 1/4 cup sugar
- 2 cups milk
- 3 eggs
- 1 tsp vanilla extract

Instructions:

1. Preheat oven to 375°F (190°C). Butter a baking dish and place prunes inside.
2. Whisk flour, sugar, milk, eggs, and vanilla until smooth.
3. Pour batter over prunes and bake for 40-45 minutes.

Salade de Fruits Frais avec Lavande (Fresh Fruit Salad with Lavender)

Ingredients:

- 1 cup strawberries, halved
- 1/2 cup blueberries
- 1/2 cup raspberries
- 1 peach, sliced
- 1 tbsp honey
- 1/2 tsp dried culinary lavender

Instructions:

1. Toss fruit with honey and lavender.
2. Let sit for 15 minutes before serving.

www.ingramcontent.com/pod-product-compliance
Lightning Source LLC
LaVergne TN
LVHW081459060526
838201LV00056BA/2827